As long as there are babies born in this world, ... If that were enough, everyone would probably be happy to a certain extent. What's missing though are real mothers like my wife, Almarie Chalmers who I have witness first hand not only putting emphasis on bringing a child into this world, but placed the most emphasis on raising a child in this world. Society's landscape is strewn with mothers who could have been great, some show amazing promises, but never reach their fullest potential. And then there are others like Almarie who went to the next level by multiplying and maximizing her talent to improve her childrens talents. If I was a child and had to chose a mother-Almarie would be second to none.

Ronnie Chalmers

"Thirty plus years as a parent, educator, coach and motivational speaker lend credence to Almarie's voice on raising positive, productive children."

P.V. Brown
The Personal Poet, Anchorage, AK

The ball is always in the your court when you are eager to learn, with right attitude, watch your trusted ones and take cues from them. Just as we have Faith in GOD .... WE must ask GOD to give us direction as the ball lands on our court. This books gives you food for thought in all of those areas of realizing the ball is in your court. Now What?

Louise Thompson
Retired Educator

Traveling the Kansas University thrilling road to the National Championship with Almarie Chalmers offers a unique viewpoint into the trials and triumphs experienced. Devoted mother-coach to Mario "the shot" Chalmers, unofficial spiritual advocate to many team members and fans, Almarie shares her experience laced with her steadfast faith in Christ and His devine influence both on and off the court. Enjoy the trip and be blessed.

Diana Low
Friend of Chalmers Family & Lawrence KS resident
President of Vision Quest Retail Strategies

THE BALL IS IN
YOUR COURT

THE BALL IS IN YOUR COURT

Embracing Your Child's Dreams

ALMARIE MOSLEY CHALMERS

Copyright © 2010 by Almarie Mosley Chalmers

All rights reserved. No part of this book may be used or reproduced in any manner whatsoever without prior written consent of the author, except as provided by the United States of America copyright law.

Published by Advantage, Charleston, South Carolina.
Member of Advantage Media Group.

ADVANTAGE is a registered trademark and the Advantage colophon is a trademark of Advantage Media Group, Inc.

Printed in the United States of America.

ISBN: 978-1-59932-213-1
LCCN: 2010913308

This publication is designed to provide accurate and authoritative information in regard to the subject matter covered. It is sold with the understanding that the publisher is not engaged in rendering legal, accounting, or other professional services. If legal advice or other expert assistance is required, the services of a competent professional person should be sought.

Advantage Media Group is proud to be a part of the Tree Neutral™ program. Tree Neutral offsets the number of trees consumed in the production and printing of this book by taking proactive steps such as planting trees in direct proportion to the number of trees used to print books. To learn more about Tree Neutral, please visit **www. treeneutral.com**. To learn more about Advantage's commitment to being a responsible steward of the environment, please visit **www. advantagefamily.com/green**

Advantage Media Group is a leading publisher of business, motivation, and self-help authors. Do you have a manuscript or book idea that you would like to have considered for publication? Please visit **www.amgbook.com** or call **1.866.775.1696**

This book is dedicated to my family:

My darling husband, Ronnie who always supported
my dreams and passions, my children, Roneka and
Mario who steadfast love is strength for the journey

My late (grand)mother, Ethel Mae Evans, whose unconditional love, acceptance, guidance and life style has
been an inspiration to continue my walk with Christ.

My late mother, Joann Davis from whom I learned
the importance of holding on to HOPE!

To my siblings and aunt who loved,
believed and supported my dreams.

My dad, Alphonso Mosley whose journey in life as a soldier
in the USArmy gives me inspiration to stay in the fight.

And most of all:

I have to a give all the glory and praise to my heavenly Father
who has inspired me on this journey as well as the many

spiritual mothers and sisters He places in my life along the way!

May God continue to bless each of you

ACKNOWLEDGEMENTS

A cknowledgements are often hard to do without the thought that someone important will be left off the list. Therefore I want to say *"thank you"* to the many spiritual mentors and friends that have spoken and supported me on the journey of raising my children.

To Pastor Lawrence, my mentor and friend for your spiritual guidance as your spoken words were always divinely inspired as you always treasured God's opinion more than your own. That is true wisdom!

To the "Sniper" Marsha Stallworth Dixson, a true prophetess from the Lord who has spoken into my life more times than I can share and the word given never returned void as it accomplished that which was divinely inspired. Thanks for believing in the dream!

To Lady Lavonne Smith and Women of Excellence, whose words of wisdom and encouragement were always a silent push to stay the course? Thanks for always believing in me when I couldn't believe in myself.

To all that contributed to the publishing of this work both in front and behind the scene your time and effort is greatly appreciated.

FOREWORD

Our mom has always instilled the importance of placing God first in our life, and to this day encourages us to find a quiet place and time to ask God about tough decisions. When we were kids, she always talked about the mustard seed of faith, a reference to one of her favorite scriptures, and she injected that into our lives. Whether it was literally her giving everyone on one of our teams a mustard seed and a laminated copy of that scripture, or one of us contemplating a career move, her advice was consistent: "Pray and ask God what He would have you do. I'll support whatever you decide to do."

She also raised us to keep that faith, even in the most troublesome or sad moments. When our grandmother died, it was tough on all of us, but my mother urged us to use it as an incentive to try even harder to reach our potential, because our grandmother would be looking down upon us, smiling, and proud.

Knowing it was okay to dream big was a huge reason why we felt we could reach our potential. Mom always encouraged us to have dreams, research what was involved in accomplishing those dreams, set up a plan and make it happen. She did that for as long as we can recall, whether it was a track meet in elementary school or a YMCA basketball team. Mom didn't just let us dream for the sake of dreaming, however she knew that every dream pursued either ends up being achieved or opens up the door to a new dream which we wouldn't recognize had we not chased all of the dreams. She allowed us to learn that when one door closes another opens, because she wasn't afraid to let us fail. She didn't *want* us to fail—and she stood and cheered us on no matter what—but she wasn't afraid to embrace our every dream even if she felt, deep down, it wouldn't directly lead to success. And when success eluded us, she would help us see that new open door and encourage us to walk through it.

At times in our lives when we've felt pressured, Mom has always been there to reassure us that staying calm, thinking clearly and doing our very best would lead to the achievement of our dreams. "Let your actions speak louder than anyone else's words," she would tell us. She took every step with us, wanting the dream to come true as much as we did. "Never," she would say, "let anyone tell you that you can't achieve what you dream."

And you know what? Mom *still* stays after us about pursuing our dreams, even ones that could have been forgotten or lost in the maze of time—dreams she knows we had as little children. Time may forget, but our mother doesn't! When she thinks we need to be reminded that there is still a dream of ours that needs pursuing—that God wants us to go after it—she lets us know in a subtle way. After all, as she likes to tell us, "God has a plan for you, and that plan does *not* include defeat."

When someone in our family achieves a goal, the individual doesn't say "I did it!". In the Chalmers family, it's "We did it!" because without our mom (and dad too!), it wouldn't have happened.

Roneka and Mario Chalmers, June 23, 2010

CONTENTS

A Fine Example

*"Example is not the main thing in influencing others.
It is the only thing."*

Albert Schweitzer

L ife would be so much easier if guarantees were part of the package. Just imagine if our children came with money-back guarantees or our marriages came with a guarantee of satisfaction.

Unfortunately, what passes for a warranty in life usually expires after a year or two, but there is one guarantee that is always valid: there is a Father in heaven who will hold you, love you and guide you through life's trials and joys.

I was five years old the first time I remember clinging to that promise. It was a beautiful Florida afternoon, and I was playing with a friend in the soft, grassy front yard as the sun smiled down upon us. My mother was at the Laundromat, or so I thought, but as we played she pulled up in her car and ran back into the house as if she had forgotten something. Moments later, we heard a loud BOOM!

I had no idea what had happened as I ran into the house, only to find my mother lying on the floor in a crumpled heap. I later learned that my mother had taken her own life. I wasn't the only one left behind—I had nine-year-old sister and a 12-month-old brother. I couldn't and didn't understand why my mother would take her own life. *What about her life was so bad that it provoked such a tragic action?* This question haunted me for years to come.

My parents were married at the time of my mother's suicide, but my father was stationed overseas in the military. Suddenly, he was an only parent, and he struggled with what to do. Taking all of us overseas with him was not ideal since he would be raising us alone. He decided to move us out of Florida, where we had lived with my mother and her parents, to his parents' home in North Carolina. As my dad drove us to our new home, it was raining, and I passed the time by counting the raindrops as they hit the windshield.

What followed was a scary time for me. I had a lot of questions, including how I would adjust to life with this "new" family. I soon realized, however, that all of the questions I had were met by unconditional love and wisdom by my grandmother, Ethel Mae, whom I called Mom. She was in her late 50s when she and her husband took us in. They had just moved to the country to enjoy their retirement, but they swiftly made the adjustments needed to raise three small children without ever making us feel as if we were burdens.

In addition to being a wife, mother and grandmother, Ethel Mae was a pastor. I have never known anyone who loved God more or better exhibited His love toward others. She was a remarkable woman who introduced me to the concept of being a Godly person. Her daily example showed me what it meant to be a victor in a life where there are no guarantees. She "walked the walk" long before that expression was popular.

I didn't realize it when I was five years old, or even 15 years old, but I know now that she was the epitome of the Proverb 31 virtuous woman.

The sayings of King Lemuel—**an oracle**
his mother taught him:

O my son, O son of my womb,
O son of my vows,
do not spend your strength on women,
your vigor on those who ruin kings.
It is not for kings, O Lemuel—
not for kings to drink wine,
not for rulers to crave beer,
lest they drink and forget what the law decrees,
and deprive all the oppressed of their rights.
Give beer to those who are perishing,
wine to those who are in anguish;
let them drink and forget their poverty
and remember their misery no more.
Speak up for those who cannot speak for themselves,
for the rights of all who are destitute.
Speak up and judge fairly;
defend the rights of the poor and needy.

Epilogue: The Wife of Noble Character

A wife of noble character who can find?
She is worth far more than rubies.
Her husband has full confidence in her

and lacks nothing of value.
She brings him good, not harm,
all the days of her life.
She selects wool and flax
and works with eager hands.
She is like the merchant ships,
bringing her food from afar.
She gets up while it is still dark;
she provides food for her family
and portions for her servant girls.
She considers a field and buys it;
out of her earnings she plants a vineyard.
She sets about her work vigorously;
her arms are strong for her tasks.
She sees that her trading is profitable,
and her lamp does not go out at night.
In her hand she holds the distaff
and grasps the spindle with her fingers.
She opens her arms to the poor
and extends her hands to the needy.
When it snows, she has no fear for her household;
for all of them are clothed in scarlet.
She makes coverings for her bed;
she is clothed in fine linen and purple.
Her husband is respected at the city gate,
where he takes his seat among the elders of the land.
She makes linen garments and sells them,
and supplies the merchants with sashes.
She is clothed with strength and dignity;
she can laugh at the days to come.
She speaks with wisdom,
and faithful instruction is on her tongue.
She watches over the affairs of her household
and does not eat the bread of idleness.
Her children arise and call her blessed;

her husband also, and he praises her:
"Many women do noble things,
but you surpass them all."
Charm is deceptive, and beauty is fleeting;
but a woman who fears the LORD is to be praised.
Give her the reward she has earned,
and let her works bring her praise at the city gate.

When I read that scripture, I can picture my grandmother in each of those scenarios. She worked so hard to make sure that our needs were met and helped the needy of the community. She was worth far more than a ton of rubies to me.

My grandmother referred to Proverbs 31 as "God's Value System," and she lived by it. I can still hear her talking to us about the virtues described therein, and being a living model, and the importance of studying it and striving to live it. This proverb was part of the advice that King Lemuel's mother gave him to use as a guide as he searched for a wife. His mother was trying to give him everyday examples of what wisdom looks like when it is applied on a continual basis. Her daughter-in-law sure had a lot to live up to, didn't she!

I'm fully aware this bit of scripture is somewhat controversial and could cause the blood to stir in women who feel we can never live up to that kind of example, and that it just adds to and fuels the pressure we deal with every day. I admit that the woman described in the passage *does* seem too good to be true: she brings home the bacon, fries it up in a pan, looks good, smells good and wears a smile the entire time. She's a perfect package, which leads some women to believe she's a figment of God's imagination, and that it's just too much to ask that we live up to her standard on days when we can barely keep it together enough to get a shower or make it to the grocery store.

I understand that point of view, but from my perspective the writer isn't trying to make us feel like slackers, but rather to show us how to live in a responsible, productive and prosperous way. The whole book of Proverbs is not so much promises of God, as it is observations and principles of how the world operates. I guess you could say it's a road map to help us navigate all of the heartbreak, sadness and stumbling blocks that we encounter in this world. There are so many things about this woman that we can emulate. If we apply even a few, we'd find much more fulfillment in our roles as mothers, wives, sisters and friends. I often find that when I strive to put the principles into practice, my life and my family seem a lot more grounded.

I wonder at times where I would be if not for the influence and example of my grandmother. Every child needs a parent who strives to be a model of values and love, but in the end, it is up to each of us to live up to that model, and we can do so by seeking wisdom from God's instruction book. He gave us examples, such as Proverbs 31, and he puts people in our lives who impart wisdom to us.

After my mother's tragic death, I felt alone in my pain for what seemed like forever. In the years since, however, I've come in contact with many people who have helped me heal. In turn,

God has allowed me to use my past to help others find comfort in their own times of grief.

We all have scars that won't go away, but life is still worth living. Even after your heart has been ripped out, there are many more miles in the journey. There are lessons to learn, relationships to embrace and joys to be celebrated.

"Being confident of this, that he who began a good work in you will carry it on to completion until the day of Christ Jesus."

Philippians 1:6

I can't mention my grandmother and her parenting style without mentioning her calm and caring way of handling our failures. That played a huge part in shaping who I am today. When one of us children would come home after doing something awful, or making a poor choice, she didn't give us a long lecture or try to make us feel guilty. Instead, she forgave us, usually over a bowl of soup, and told us that "life goes on and I will always love you." She was showing us the embodiment of Agape—a true love that includes forgiveness.

I have worked hard to practice my grandmother's model of true love when my children have disappointed me. But, again, she gave me a foundation to know *how* to put that into practice.

"She is like the merchant ships, bringing her food from afar.
She gets up while it is still dark; she provides food for her family
and portions for her servant girls. She considers a field and buys it;
out of her earnings she plants a vineyard. She sets about her work vigorously;
her arms are strong for her tasks. She sees that her trading is profitable,
and her lamp does not go out at night."

Proverbs 31:14-18

My grandmother passed on an entrepreneurial spirit to her children and grandchildren, and she was a model of grace in doing so. When she would fall down in her endeavors, she would get right back up, and she required the same of us. No matter what, she always gave God credit for her success. That is more profound to me now that she is gone and lives on through those that remain. We all have a piece of her in us, and we pass it on through actions and words to our children and to others in our lives.

Sometimes I look back and wonder how she did it. She lived to be 97, and in that long lifetime she lost three husbands, watched two children die, put another daughter through dental school and raised three grandchildren—all before she retired. Even more amazing is the fact that she made sure we all graduated from college. I can still see her sitting in her favorite chair, patting her thigh, humming and praying as she sought divine guidance. She'd go to her quiet place and get strengthened through stillness and prayer. I saw many of those prayers answered in my lifetime.

I will always love and remember my grandmother as my mother, but I will always miss knowing my birth mother. When I was growing up no one really talked about her. It wasn't until I graduated from high school that my father gave me my first and only tangible piece of her. I remember receiving it like it was yesterday. I went to visit my father after graduation, and he excused himself to the back room. When he returned he pulled out what to me was a treasure: two photographs of my mother. I still have them in my wallet. She gave me life, and I'll never know why she took her own, but she started me on this journey. I only wish she could have seen the rest of the trip.

Although I will always have questions about what happened to my mother, I learned that God has a plan for you no matter your age. He puts young lives in our paths to impact, and gives us children to emulate His love as we use His road map, Proverbs 31, to find our way through this beautiful, and sometimes painful life.

My childhood shaped who I am today and how I raised my own children. As I share my journey with you, know that I understand that we all have hurts and scars, but I truly believe we can use them to impact the lives of others, especially our children.

LOVING

"Making the decision to have a child is momentous. It is to decide forever to have your heart go walking around outside your body."

Elizabeth Stone

As a teenager, I was in love with the idea of becoming a career woman. Sometimes I'd envision my future and see myself wearing a black power suit with matching pumps or a sharply creased Air Force uniform. It wasn't a matter of *what* I was going to do, but rather that I *was* going to make it big in this world. And I was going to do it without little children dragging me down.

My grandmother had other ideas for me—all born out of love, of course. She gently pushed me toward teaching or nursing because, as she put it, those were "good careers for moms." No one seemed to understand that I had much bigger dreams. At the time, I didn't understand that God had grander plans for me far beyond what my grandmother or I could have even imagined. Looking back, I now realize that every relationship and experience gradually allowed me to see God's plan for me take shape.

As I discovered who I was becoming and where life was taking me day by day, my relationship with my sister, Joallo, played a very important role. Unknowingly, she introduced me to a person who would forever change everything about my life. One of her best friends was a boy named Ronnie. I was unimpressed by Ronnie when we first met as teenagers, but I realized after several months that I had made an impression on him.

Ronnie was three years older than me—I was just in ninth grade—when he passed me a note saying he'd like to take me on a date. I thought he had some nerve—he was an old man compared to me!—and I was more interested in playing basketball than I was in boys, so I ignored the note. Ronnie was persistent, however, and after numerous attempts on his part, I finally accepted one of his offers and we attended his prom together. I'm sure that I begged my grandmother to let me go, and she relented. In retrospect, she probably didn't want to let me go, but as I learned myself years later, it's difficult to say "no" to your children, especially when their heart is set on something. (It's not impossible, and sometimes it *is* best to just say "no.")

> *"If you, then, though you are evil, know how to give good gifts to your children, how much more will your Father in heaven give good gifts to those who ask Him!"*
>
> ———
>
> *Matthew 7:10*

Soon after that prom, Ronnie graduated, joined the Air Force and was stationed in Boston. I stayed behind in North Carolina for the next three years, finished high school, played basketball and dated Ronnie when he would come back home for visits. After graduation, I accepted a basketball scholarship to Winston Salem State in North Carolina. I was on my way to fulfilling my dreams.

By the middle of my freshman year at Winston Salem, however, I felt like I was in the wrong place. Around the same time, Ronnie was transferred to Pope Air Force Base in North Carolina, so I decided to transfer to Methodist College in nearby Fayetteville. Yes, Ronnie had finally won my heart, and we decided to get married. We were elated, but that sentiment didn't necessarily spill over to other people. My schooling was a priority for my grandmother, and she sternly told Ronnie, "You got her out of school. You keep her in school and make sure she finishes."

I continued to attend school on a basketball scholarship while Ronnie worked for the Air Force and took a part-time job at the local hospital. We were happy living in our own home, enjoying our freedom as a young married couple. It was true love and I couldn't imagine being happier. Now, I had someone to conquer the world with me.

A few months into our marriage, I noticed that my body was changing. Something felt different. I'm sure you've heard stories of women who were pregnant and didn't realize it and thought to yourself, "How is that possible? How can you *not* know you're pregnant?" Well, I was on one of those oblivious pregnant women. It just never crossed mind, probably because

I had a vision of myself that certainly did *not* include chasing around a diaper-clad baby. It sounds incredible, I know, but it took me five months to realize I was pregnant, and when I did, talk about a shock! What in the world was I going to do with a baby?

(handwritten margin note: Do we have our own plans and God changes them?)

> *"Many are the plans in a man's heart, but it is the Lord's purpose that prevails."*
>
> *Proverbs 19:21*

I had no desire whatsoever to be a mother at that time in my life, a fact I'm sure that had something to do with my own mother's suicide and absence from my life. My ideal world did not involve hauling children to basketball practice or to the dentist. That was fine for other women, but not me. I was focused on toting that beautiful black leather briefcase to an office where I had a vibrant career. Little did I know that God had begun a necessary healing process by giving me a special gift that Ronnie and I consider one of the greatest blessings ever, bestowed upon us. At the beginning of my junior year of college, our little Roneka was born. From the beginning, my love for her unfolded easily and emotions that I had never felt before came flooding out.

(handwritten margin note: God's love for us!)

During those early days of motherhood, I began to understand how God, my Father in heaven, truly cared for me and all of us as His children. It can be difficult to comprehend a power that wants to protect us and love us even more than we do our own children. God's word pertaining to the deep love for children suddenly became real to me. By experiencing this new way to love as a mother, I was able to further understand the depth of God the Father's love for me.

"How great is the love the Father has lavished on us, that we should be called children of God! And that is what we are!"

I John 3:1

This new, intense love was something that I wanted everyone around me to share, and they did. Roneka was the first grandchild among me and my siblings, and it was exciting to share her and to see others delight in her, too. With joy, fear, confusion, and determination now swirling in me, I realized now more than ever it was necessary to finish school. I also realized that was now a greater challenge.

I sat out of school during Roneka's first year with us, but then I went back and continued to play basketball and take classes for three more years. It wasn't easy, but I was determined to create the best life possible for our family. Sometimes Roneka even went to class with me, and sometimes she would stay with my friends in the dorm. She was a trooper. I can still see her cheering me on in the stands during basketball practice and games.

As invigorating as all of this was, life was far from perfect. In addition to the challenge of completing school under new circumstances, Ronnie and I also had to contend with serious health problems for Roneka. Seemingly out of nowhere, our precious baby would have vicious respiratory attacks that required us to rush her to the hospital for rounds of shots just to get her breathing under control. Night after night, I would pray that God would protect Roneka because often, the doctors were not sure she would survive the attacks. It was determined that Roneka had severe asthma, and my heart ached for my child as she suffered. If you are a mother, you're familiar with that ache—an internal gnawing at your heart that leaves a lump in your throat and your eyes all teary.

It took a couple of years and a big change for our family before Roneka's health crisis was under control. It wasn't the solution I had in mind, but my Father's loving way is not always my way. After I graduated from college, Ronnie was transferred to Elmendorf Air Force Base in Anchorage, Alaska. What was God thinking? We had no family in Alaska, and as any school-child can tell you, it's cold there! I was pulled between the idea of the adventure of living in Alaska and wanting to stay in the comfort zone where my family lived. So many tears were shed the day we drove off with our U-Haul in tow that I could only wonder what good could come of it all.

After several days of driving, as we approached the top of the continental United States, we passed by a group of beautiful wild horses. I was immediately taken by the freedom in their graceful gallops. I didn't know it at the time, but our family was about to experience a beautiful freedom of its own. After settling into our new home, I understood that my loving Father had moved us to this cool, clear-air climate so that my daughter

Has God ever taken you out of your comfort Place

could be free of her awful asthma attacks. Roneka's condition greatly improved, and she was able to live a normal life. The emergency room was no longer our second home.

What love God shows us! My Father in heaven found us a new place to live and gave our family a new lease on life! When I realized what He had done, it was an awesome moment of knowing how, in His wisdom, God gives us perfect guidance. I may not have prayed to live among snow, ice, moose and bears, but God had indeed loved us enough to move us to Alaska.

"For I know the plans I have for you," declares
the Lord, "plans to prosper you and not to harm
you, plans to give you hope and a future."

Jeremiah 29:11

The sun shines nearly 24 hours a day during the summer in Alaska, and that's how I felt about the momentous impact the move had on all of our lives. It gave us all a fresh start in a new place where new memories and traditions of our own could evolve, and it helped me deal with my emotional ailments as well. I still carried painful wounds from my childhood that needed healing. God helped me to grow as a woman, mother and wife by giving me a child to love. Yes, I may always wonder why my mother chose to die when my sister, brother and I were so young, but God gave me a chance to *be* the mother I had always dreamed of *having*. And I was determined to be the best mom I could be.

The dramatic change in my attitude toward being a mother made me think that often we try to protect ourselves, but go about it all wrong, as if we are in control of what happens in our world. Maybe we are scared of rejection and so we steer clear of close relationships because we fear they'll end badly. In my case, before I became a mother, I wouldn't let myself think about how happy it could make me because of the tragic experience of my own mother. Thank goodness that God is in control and loves us enough to help us confront our fears and failures.

Even though I was blessed to have a great mom in my grand-mother (and later even a stepmother), my childhood never came close to what I imagined my life would have been with my biological mom. Of course, I know even under ideal con-ditions that there are no guarantees, but as adults, we let our minds wander and dream about "what could have been." These scenarios are seldom good for your emotional well-being, but I felt as if God was giving me a chance to re-create what I had imagined it would be like to feel my mother's love.

With God's guidance, I have always worked extra hard at making the relationship between my daughter and me something special for both of us. Although not always perfect, being able to experience the love of being a mother has been truly healing, and has been God's way of showing me how much He loves me and wants me to be whole.

"But for you who revere my name, the sun of righteousness
will rise with healing in its wings. And you will go
out and leap like calves released from the stall."

Malachi 4:2

Thirty years after her birth, my wondrous journey as Roneka's mother continues. I am blessed to count her as my daughter and as my friend, even if we don't always agree on things, and even if I insist on telling her what she *needs* to hear rather than what she *wants* to hear. That is part of loving the children whom God places in our lives. No one wants to be the "bad parent" who says "no," but down the road the parent and child usually see that the "no" was love, protecting them from what could have been a bad situation.

I am so thankful for the gift that God gave me in Roneka so that my healing could begin. When I opened my eyes to God's grace and realized what He was doing in my life, I learned to be content with my life as a mother and wife, to relish God's love for me, and accept that I could not—and didn't need to—know what He had in store for me. Of course, with God's goodness, comes His testing of our faith.

One evening, about seven years after Roneka was born, I suddenly had debilitating abdominal pains. I was rushed to the emergency room and the doctor in the emergency room determined I was suffering from an ectopic pregnancy, with complications that were life-threatening. So much blood had seeped into my stomach that I needed immediate surgery. You can imagine the terror that raced through my mind as the worst case scenarios danced around in my head. *What if I die? What if I leave my daughter without a mom to love her?* My biggest fear was staring me right in the face. Didn't God love me? Why was this happening?

Just before the surgery, I asked my husband to phone my grandmother and ask her to pray for me. She did, and I felt the calming power of her faith and love.

As they whisked me into surgery, the doctor told me that I would certainly lose one fallopian tube, maybe both of them, and that the chances of my ever having another baby were slim. Even though I knew the surgery was a matter of life or death, I was crushed by this news. Until that moment, I hadn't given much thought to having another child, but upon hearing those words, I realized I loved being a mom and I wasn't ready to stop at one child. Apparently, God wasn't either.

After the surgery, the doctor told me that he had not been forced to remove either of my tubes, and that the blockage had been squeezed out. Keep in mind that this was at a time when medicine was not as advanced as it is today. (Back then the procedure involved much larger incisions, while now it can be done laparoscopically and with little invasion.) The doctor was astonished by the result, and I was thrilled. However, he discouraged another pregnancy, especially in the near future, until he had a chance to see how the scar tissue healed. But I was alive and full of hope.

Two years went by without any more health problems before Ronnie and I decided we would try to have another child. We knew it was a risk, but we held fast to faith in God's plan. Nine months later, with no complications, we were blessed with a baby boy we named Almario (Mario). By this time Roneka was nine, and it was exciting to watch her see God give our family a special blessing. Once again, we saw that God is good and that He never reneges on his word.

"So shall My word be that goes forth out of My mouth: it shall not return to Me void without producing any effect, useless, but it shall accomplish that which I please and purpose, and it shall prosper in the thing for which I sent it."

Isaiah 55:11

Almost three years after nearly losing my own life and the ability to bring a new one into the world, I had a baby boy whom I knew was a true miracle and gift from God. My bond with Mario was different from the beginning. He was the apple of our entire family's eye. Ronnie, Roneka and I had endured a long road from ectopic pregnancy, through the long period of healing, to the pregnancy with Mario, and having a healthy child. We all knew Mario was truly an answer to much prayer.

Little Mario was determined to show the world he had powerful lungs. He could scream and cry so loud that the doctor suggested that perhaps Mario would be a great singer one day. In a way, the doctor was right. Mario did become a performer, but he uses his powerful lungs to help him expand his energy on the basketball court rather than on a Broadway stage!

In very different ways, and for very different reasons, my children are a constant reminder of how God answers our prayers and how deep His love is for us. My two unique paths to motherhood have shown me how He tests us and then rewards us when we obey Him. He has the answers, He knows the way, and sometimes we make the mistake of moving forward ourselves, without His help. But, oh, the pain we avoid when we allow our Father to guide us in His unconditional love.

Loving our children through the happy times is easy, but tough times test our love. It is so much easier when children do as they are told, because as mothers (parents) we know the challenges that await them in this world. We know if they would only listen to us life would be so much better for them! It is a tough pill to swallow when we realize that God feels the same way in His love—why don't we just listen to Him!

As I was writing this chapter, I searched my mind for a story to share about a time when unconditional love came into play. Unfortunately, a fresh example presented itself at that very moment, and it became the subject of newspaper articles and sports talk shows across the nation.

It was a Wednesday morning in the first week of September 2008, and Mario was attending the Rookie Transition Camp in New York. The idea behind the camp is to help new NBA players navigate the road of fame and fortune. As anyone who follows professional sports knows, life at that level can be riddled with drugs and other negative influences. The camp is designed in part to help young NBA players avoid that trouble.

At about 9 AM I received a text message informing me that Mario was being sent home from the camp. My initial reaction was that he must be ill or had sustained an injury. However, I quickly shifted from worry to anger as I learned that in the wee hours of Wednesday morning, he was in the room of a teammate from college. There were some girls in the room with them, and that was a big deal, because the rules are clear that girls, cell phones, families and friends are strictly off-limits at the camp.

At this point, I was heavy-hearted. How many times had I shared the stories of Sampson and Delilah with Mario, or told him to be wary of the hirelings that come along to distract us from staying focused? Did he not hear anything I said? Had we come this far just for him to do something so careless? It appeared at that moment that he'd forgotten all of those childhood lessons.

It is in bittersweet moments like these that you want to take a hard line with your child, but at the same time, you want to give them a huge hug. Of course you wonder if either of those things will help, and then you have to deal with the situation at hand.

In the moment, I asked the Lord to show me what the lesson was in all of this. God uses these tests to teach not only the parties directly involved, but others as well. As a mom, I was sad, mad and disgusted at what happened and what was reported.

It was another situation, among many, where I hung my hopes on the simple creed, "This too shall pass." The debacle did, however, give me a chance to once again talk with Mario about making the best choice when he is thrust into compromising situations. I stressed the need to stand on what he knows to be true and to remember that character counts, especially in the moments when you are tested.

During the days following the incident, many mothers let me know that I was not alone and that their hearts went out to me. Words of encouragement and prayers poured in and helped me to cope. Many of these mothers not only prayed with me, but also shared stories about times when their children had been found in disappointing situations. In all of this, we agreed that bad choices and heartbreaking actions on the part of our children make for hard lessons, but that life goes on.

It was such a relief to find mothers who understood my heartache were willing to lend their encouragement to me through this trial. Difficult times as a parent are always going to come, and it is not always easy to like your children when they pull stunts like this one on you. But if we model our heavenly Father's love for us, it makes the pain far less substantial and easier to accept.

In my heart I know that regardless of the fact that we as humans look at the outside and what is most readily apparent, God looks at the inside, to the heart. Mario has a good heart and he is a good son. He is human, and like all of us he errs from time to time. I constantly pray that God continues to keep him as he grows into the man he is designed to become. But it is important to make wise choices and to do the right thing. We have to be willing to find out the root of problem before the change can come.

DISCOVERING & EDUCATING

"We are all born with wonderful gifts. We use these gifts to express ourselves, to amuse, to strengthen, and to communicate. We begin as children to explore and develop our talents, often unaware that we are unique, that not everyone can do what we're doing!"

Lynn Johnston

When he was a preschooler, we knew that Mario loved basketball. Even when he didn't have a basketball in his hand, he pretended to shoot an imaginary ball. We didn't know at the time that his obsession with bouncing a ball would turn out to be his career. As he got older, Mario's passion for the game never wavered, so we explored options that would help him discover if he wanted to seriously pursue basketball, or if it was just a passing childhood phase. We enrolled him in camps, summer teams and clinics, and he still loved the game and was good at it. When we saw weaknesses in his game, we made it a point to help him improve in those areas.

In high school, Mario was as passionate as ever about basketball and we did everything we could to help him become a better player in the hope that he might be able to play college ball. We never told him that his dream to play professional basketball was an impossible one. He definitely had a rare talent and we knew that we should help him develop it, but we made certain that he understood that basketball was not life, and that his studies were important, too. I guess you could say we were cautious with him about the odds of being able to play professional basketball while also encouraging him to pursue that dream.

Had Mario not been good at basketball, but still had a desire to play professionally, it would have been poor parenting on our part to follow the path we did. But I felt sure God had blessed Mario with a skill and talent, and that we as his parents were doing the right thing. With Mario, the right path was obvious for the most part, but sometimes a child wants to chase a dream that you, as a parent, honestly believe is beyond their grasp. In those cases, you can only turn it over to God, pray about it with your child and, instead of stomping out their light, redirect their vision to areas where you see talent. It's all a process of discovering who they are and giving them the education to learn more about who and what they want to become. If they like to dance, enroll them in a class. If they like crafts, take them to an art class. If they like pictures, help them learn photography. Then, help them use their talent to help others and to acclaim God, because it is He who has given all of us talents and the honor, as parents, to help nurture them.

"We have different gifts, according to the grace given us."

Romans 12:6

When our children are young they seem to discover something new every day. It's so much fun to help them learn to write their names or tie their shoes, but as they get older, we sometimes lose sight of the many wonderful things they have yet to discover and learn.

I can recall many times in my life when other people helped me "teach" life lessons to Roneka and Mario. God puts certain people in our lives to help us be better women and mothers. We may not realize it until after the fact, but some of these people change our course and the course of our children. As a result, it's important to watch who we let into our "village of influence," because the villagers play a vital role in educating our children. We need to make sure all of the villagers have the right motives and pure hearts. We should not take lightly where and to whom we hand over our children. As mothers, part of our role is to be a sentry at the access points of our children's lives.

"The tongue has the power of life and death, and those who love it will eat its fruit."

Proverbs 18:21

The first step toward your child's divine purpose being fulfilled is an environment where they can develop a strong character. How do we do this? How do we keep out naysayers, antagonists and those who would harm our children? First, we commit our children to God and ask Him to watch over and care for them. God knows it isn't always going to be a pretty trip down

Parenting Lane, but He has the roadmap. If we stop and ask Him for directions we might have a smoother ride.

I can't begin to tell you the number of times that I have not taken time to read the map and gotten lost on the journey of raising two children. I've been discouraged and impatient at times, and felt I wasn't living up to my potential as a mother. God is the one who bestowed the precious gift of our children upon us, and if we let Him, He will help us find joy and peace in the parenting process. In those moments when we temporarily forget God, we are reminded that we are not in control of our lives.

In order to discover what God's will is for our children and ourselves, we have to continually pray and ask for guidance. I truly believe that Jesus wants us to be as concerned for our children's well-being as He is with ours. We must pray for our children every day, just as Jesus prays to the Father for us.

"Who is he that condemns? Christ Jesus, who died—
more than that, who was raised to life—is at the right
hand of God and is also interceding for us."

Romans 8:34

The second step in helping your children fulfill their divine purpose is to never stop building a loving, positive village around them. When they go to visit a friend or relative, are they seeing things on television or playing violent video games that you wouldn't allow? Or are you putting your children in places where there are adults who will encourage them and hold them to the value system that you teach?

The process of helping our children learn their purpose in life starts when they are infants, when even at such a tender age they start to notice their environment and the influences around them. Who has influence over your child? Are they the role models you want for your son or daughter?

The third step: As you surround your children with the right influences, you also help them explore their passions. Self-discovery of the gifts they possess is the beginning of a wonderful journey for your children. Watching them play and enjoy various activities can help you identify their passions right along with them. Take notice of what they do without effort or just for the fun of it, the things they do beyond what family members think they should or because you as their parent did. Let each child be their own person. Enjoy the journey of discovering their passions. These passions are something that will be with them for a lifetime and can help them live their life with great joy.

> *"Nothing great in the world has been*
> *accomplished without passion."*
>
> *George Hegel*

The fourth step: We need to allow children to explore a variety of activities, even though they may not stick with all of them forever, or even a year, or a few weeks. By doing this, they can discover their strengths and learn lessons that might otherwise go untaught. I learned that whenever my children delved into new activities and organizations, I needed to make sure that the adults in the program had values and morals that lined up with what we were teaching at home. If they did not, we would move on and find a program that did.

> *"Do not be deceived and misled! Evil companionships corrupt and deprave good manners and morals and character."*
>
> *I Corinthians 15:33*

Let me add to the notion of variety in experiences, by saying that we should offer experiences to our children that go beyond their own needs, such as giving back to others on the mission fields or in community service projects. To be able to experience serving others within their own community is far more valuable than the child will ever know in the moment.

The fifth step: In our own lives we should strive to be a role model for our children to emulate. We cannot expect public figures to do that for us. Famous people will always leave impressions on our youth, but as parents you hope that they will emulate you, because they consistently observed the right thing being done, and saw the results. Providing a model in what you do, as well as what you say, becomes even more important when you remember a small person is watching you. What will you model for them? I reflect on a conversation with Mario, when he referred to me as a passive driver, because I showed no reaction when other drivers did things that would upset many people. I explained that there was nothing to gain but a headache by getting upset. He insisted that when another driver cuts you off you should "stare them down." He learned that behavior by watching another driver, whose name I won't mention. This is a good example of how children put more stock in what you do than what you say. So model what you teach! No, we are not going to be perfect, but if at the end of the road you can see that what you've modeled has been copied, you'll have made an impact.

> "Train up a child in the way he should go, [and in keeping with his individual gift or bent], and when he is old he will not depart from it."
>
> ———————
>
> Proverbs 22:6

As we model the behavior, beliefs and values that we stand on, we also need to speak "life" into all situations with our words. What I mean by that, is that we must guard against using our tongue as a sword, and use it instead as a teaching tool. We've all heard the old saying, "Sticks and stones may break my bones, but words will never hurt me," but the reality is that hurtful words can scar for a lifetime. Words spoken in truth, although sometimes hurtful, can evolve into a growing experience for our child. But words spoken thoughtlessly and in haste can run on an endless loop in a child's mind, playing the same negative message over and over and over.

We've all been around children who can't seem to do anything right, so consider this: if a child is told by his mother that he is "bad," he is going to take her words to mean that he is a bad person. In this situation, it is better to tell the child that his behavior is bad, not that he's a bad child. The appropriate handling of these types of situations helps the child discover that they need to change their behavior, and in turn, they've learned a valuable lesson.

Let me share four invaluable lessons I've learned along the road of mothering:

great lesson

1. **Take time to communicate and listen:** Talk about your lives and ask questions of each other. You can start this process by scheduling a once-a-week sit down with your child during which you ask each other questions as simple as "How was your week?" or "What went well for you this week?" In order to draw out more than a "Yes" or "No" answer, you can add questions such as "What would you change about your week?" Make sure to involve your husband and other siblings as well. Take time to listen to what is really being said.

2. **Take time to support:** Most of us wouldn't miss the many sporting events or dance recitals in our children's lives, but what about the weeknight spelling test, study sessions or sobbing over a broken heart or lost relationship? These small moments are times when we can really teach valuable lessons and encourage our children. There are also times when we must show tough love and let them know

that it's alright to say "No." Encourage them to be themselves.

3. **Take time to relax:** As mothers we know that life's journey can be long and offer little rest. We are better people when we take time to relax and recharge. This is a lesson we can model and it helps to maintain a peaceful home.

> *"The Lord will fight for you; and you shall hold your peace and remain at rest."*
>
> *Exodus 14:14*

4. **Take time to pray and read:** We've all heard the saying "a family who prays together, stays together." It may be cliché, but I believe it. I can remember times as a young mother when I would lift myself up or others in need with my prayer, but I remember even more fondly those times when we, as a family, would lift our requests and praises to God. Many times it was as simple as saying "The Lord's Prayer" together, but it was an opportunity to show our children the power of prayer. By taking time to pray daily with our children, we model the power of prayer and show that it's okay to be bold in prayer and in faith. Remember this may be the only time that you have this sphere of influence to impact their lives. This can only be helpful as they get older and

don't consistently have prayerful influences around them.

Ask yourself these questions: Are you leading by example when it comes to continual growing and learning? Are you using your talents in the way that you should? Before we can expect to help our children discover their own talents, we must explore our own God-given gifts and dreams. I remember being a young wife, sitting with my husband in church one Sunday when our minister asked the two of us to stand up. At first, Ronnie and I both thought it was a little weird because he said, "Don't think it strange as you travel in various places across the nation, as this will be your ministry." We didn't have a clue what he was talking about, but he was speaking to what God had called us to do. As the years went on, we realized that we are here to impact the lives of young people, wherever we were planted.

God had a divine plan for us, but being stubborn human beings, we had to learn to embrace the journey. There were so many times that we wanted to run from situations God placed us in, but we learned along the way that running doesn't solve the problem, because when you stop running, the problem is still waiting for you.

So true

One of the best things for us about following God's plan is that He saw fit to include our children on the journey. While we were working with them to discover their strengths and talents, we were able to help other children do the same. God used both my and Ronnie's basketball backgrounds to help us realize our ministry.

When Roneka was old enough to play competitive basketball, Ronnie and I embraced the chance to coach a group of wonderful young ladies from the Anchorage and Wasilla communities. We didn't know that we were starting a journey that would help us discover God's plan for our family's life. It was a wonderful experience that allowed us to get to know other parents and to share our experiences on the court and in life with that team of girls.

On one occasion, we traveled with the team to a tournament in Cincinnati. Those girls from Alaska got a chance to show that they could compete on the basketball court, but they also experienced life outside of the Alaskan borders, something not many of them had done. It was a special feeling to know that God was using us to change these girls' lives. We starting seeing God's plan for us that had been revealed in church years before. He really did have bigger ideas for us, that would take us across the nation. And what a blessing that our children got to see us discover a way to use our own talents and cultivate theirs at the same time. God's journey of learning never ends.

EMBRACING THE DREAM

*"I have learned, that if one advances confidently in the direction
of his dreams, and endeavors to live the life he has imagined,
he will meet with a success unexpected in common hours."*

Henry David Thoreau

When my children were younger we would visit my family back in North Carolina each summer. On Sunday mornings we would go with my grandmother to the church where she pastored. During the service, she would call all of the kids in the congregation to the altar for children's time, and ask them to lay their dreams before God, so that the congregation could pray over them. Little Mario would say the same thing every Sunday: "I want to play basketball like Michael Jordan." Chuckles and snickers could be heard from the audience when my grandmother asked him if he was sure that he wouldn't rather be a preacher. In his tiny pre-school voice, he would tell her that he would preach on the basketball courts. Even though we all found his dream to be cute and a little on the big side, we all prayed over Mario's dream, for it was a dream from his heart.

Now that Mario is playing on the same courts where Michael Jordan played, I am so glad that I listened to that still, small voice that told me to encourage Mario and not to burst his bubble by telling him that he should choose a more realistic career. Honestly, I secretly hoped he would become a lawyer, but he never wavered in his passion. I admit that in my head I thought, "Yeah, right, what boy doesn't want to be like Mike?" But in my heart, I wanted him to reach his goal.

In July 2008, just weeks after Mario signed with the NBA, I was back at that same North Carolina church. It was amazing that so many people remembered those Sundays when Mario would dream aloud, and they said they believe that we were all being taught the lesson that nothing is impossible with God. Please note that you have to do some work as well!

"For with God nothing is ever impossible."

Luke 1:37

"But Jesus looked at them, and said, with men this is impossible; but all things are possible with God."

Matthew 19:26

Often when I am at basketball games, I am approached by mothers who ask how we helped Mario achieve his dream. The answer is that we embraced it along with him. When we realized that he was serious about playing basketball and his talent was obvious, we did everything we could to make sure he was surrounded by opportunities that would enhance his basketball skills.

Now, embracing that dream with him was definitely an easier-said-than-done proposition. We have been to, coached and cheered at more basketball games than I could count in another lifetime. There were days when we all wanted to throw in the towel—and throw it at each other. However, the biggest reason the dream never died was that I learned to seek God's guidance and to pray without cessation when it came to what, at times, seemed like an impossible pursuit.

Chasing and embracing your child's dream may not look anything like my family's path. Your child may want to go to the Olympics, be a great composer, the next Monet or even a CPA. It's up to you as a parent to help them see what that goal will look like when it is reached, and what it will take to get there. I truly believe God has given each of us a talent, and it is just as important for you to embrace your child's talent as it is for them.

Sometimes society makes it difficult to live outside of the norm when it comes to embracing dreams. Parents, friends and family have expectations of children, such as becoming a doctor or lawyer, instead of chasing a dream of, say, being an artist. It can seem so risky, and it can be risky, but if God is in charge, He promises to see us through.

Our daughter, Roneka, played basketball, too, but her dream was to become a lawyer. As her mother, I didn't think a law career was a good fit for Roneka. However, I supported her dream while continuing to encourage her creative side. When she was young, not a day went by when she didn't draw or design clothes for paper dolls. She loved it, and I have to say, she was good at it. Once she started college, Roneka quickly realized law school was not for her, and she began talking about becoming a fashion designer or a buyer. In a light bulb moment, Roneka realized her dream had been her passion all along.

When Roneka graduated from college, she headed for one of the nation's most upscale department stores. Soon thereafter, she became one of the youngest managers in the store, and continually relocated for the company to open stores in various part of the country, often reaching sales goals that were said to be unreachable. Roneka is still reaching for big dreams in the fashion industry, and I am still sitting on the sidelines praying for her. I often remind her of what God can do when you work hard, stay determined and continually ask Him for guidance.

"Delight yourself also in the Lord: and He will give you the desires and secret petitions of your heart."

Psalm 37:4

When I look back at the small dreams my children had growing up, I realize that my embracing of them was as important as the children having them. I think about Roneka dreaming of winning the shiny, blue bicycle that would go to the winner of her elementary school's Jessie Owens Track and Field Day. At the time, her asthma was giving her a few problems, but she wanted that bike more than anything. We practiced, timed her and supported her in the time leading up to the field day when she would race for the bike.

The big day came and as she lined up to begin the race, her father and I gave her words of encouragement: "Don't worry about what is going on to the left or right, just stay focused on the front. Lean forward as you approach the finish line." With those last-minute instructions swirling in her head, she stepped up to the starting line, and as the start gun sounded, she did all of the things we talked about. As the finish line neared, there were several other little girls running neck and neck with her. However, Roneka leaned forward at the finish and won. The bike was hers. Her dream had come true not by wishing and hoping, but through hard work, determination, focus and, as always, a little prayer.

I also sometimes think about the time when Mario was a freshman in high school and a little unsure of himself as an underclassman. His skills and drive led the coaching staff, which included my husband, to tell Mario to try out for the varsity team. He made it as the back-up point guard, and then the starting point guard transferred to a new school, leaving the position open for Mario. It was a great opportunity for Mario that exceeded his dreams. In fact, that year the team won the state championship. They did it again the next year, too. What an accomplishment, but would it have happened at all if we hadn't nudged him to try out for the varsity team as a freshman?

Like the rest of us, Mario has had setbacks while chasing his dream. His junior year in high school, his team lost the championship on a Hail Mary shot by the opposing team at the buzzer. His senior year was even tougher, when the challenge of playing with an inexperienced team led to fifth place in the state. We all felt a letdown at the end of that season, but we didn't give up on a college basketball career. Mario's hard work paid off when he was invited to play in the McDonald's All-American Game, a dream he had talked about for years.

Looking back at Mario's path to reaching his dream, I see God's hand in our lives in so many situations, guiding us and giving us strength to continue. No, Mario isn't Michael Jordan by any means, but he has accomplished a huge part of his dream through hard work, determination, focus and many prayers on his behalf. He realizes that he doesn't have to be Mike, but rather he can take that which was modeled by a great athlete like Jordan and make his own place on the court.

It was not by luck or chance that he went to the University of Kansas on a basketball scholarship, or that he hit the three-pointer that sent the 2008 NCAA Championship Game into overtime (when Kansas eventually won over Memphis), or that he was then drafted by the Miami Heat. His success came because we all embraced his dream. We believed in him and had faith that God placed him in our care so that we could see him through to his dream.

That being said, I know that not all dreams come true. The Bible tells us that in Romans 8:28: *"And we know that all things work together for good to them that love God, to them who are the called according to his purpose."* As parents, we have to help our children, and ourselves, find the lesson when our dreams seem to be falling apart. Was it God's dream? Were we pursuing the right dream? If not, redirect, refocus and find the path you are meant to travel.

"Set your minds on things above, not on earthly things."

Colossians 3:2

Life has offered many dreams for my children, and many times they have faced the agony of defeat. I pray daily that there are many more dreams to come true for both of them. I encourage you to do the same each day as you pray for your children.

What about our own dreams as parents? Dreams for parents can sometimes get lost in the midst of raising a family, driving to soccer practice and trying to fit it all in. We were all like our children once, with goals and dreams, some reached and some left hanging out there. Take time to think about the dreams you held in your heart as a child or young adult and share those with your children as they grow. I look back and feel satisfied with the dreams of my younger years. I wanted to play basketball, check; win a division championship, check; graduate from college, check.

Even though I was happy with my young family, I realized that I still had dreams within me that I wanted to reach. In working toward accomplishing some of those dreams, I felt as if I was showing my children that you should never stop dreaming, even if the dreams change. No, I wasn't working on Wall Street as I had dreamed of doing as a young girl, but I had new dreams that I was even more excited about.

One of my dreams became reality after 20 years of teaching at the elementary, middle, high school and college levels. I had a dream of starting my own business, and I did so in Alaska after Roneka left for college. God gave me the opportunity to turn my desire, to give young female basketball players a safe and nurturing environment to learn the game, into a reality. I established the Hi-Rise Sports Camp, the first all girls basketball camp in Alaska. Through the camp we were able to provide dozens of girls an opportunity to train and prepare for competitive basketball. It was an awesome feeling to realize this dream and to know that God had been preparing me for this reality, through his gift of challenges I had faced and jobs I had held throughout my life.

Like many others, I also dreamed of writing a book. During this time of starting my own business, I was able to pursue my writing. Not knowing much about the publishing business, I self-published a small book that gave me a way to reach others and to share with them how God had worked in my life. While I had always hoped to expand upon my first book, it wasn't until more years and experiences had passed that my preparation finally met opportunity.

I am so grateful to God that He has allowed me to accomplish the desires of my heart in the midst of raising a family; working and helping my children reach their dreams. As mothers, we celebrate the accomplishments of our children with great joy, and I am sure that we can all share stories of the successes of our children. I just want to encourage you to embrace the dreams of your children, whether it is a big career, running for class president, winning a bike or making a team. We must encourage them to dream outside of the box.

I am so thankful for my grandmother who allowed me to dream and who told me that no dream was a bad dream or an impossible dream. I guess I have her to thank for giving me the guidance that would eventually lead me to embrace my children's dreams. She knew that we all have something to give the world. Although she did not live to see Mario's dream come true, she always believed in his dream to "be like Mike."

Through my grandmother's eyes, my children's eyes and my own eyes, I have come to define dreaming as never underestimating the importance of having and keeping the faith.

"A faithful man shall abound with blessings."

Proverbs 28:20

He replied, "Because you have so little faith, I tell you the truth, if you have faith as small as a mustard seed you can say to this mountain, move from here to there and it will move. Nothing will be impossible for you."

Matthew 17:20

I encourage you to allow your children to dream the impossible dream, offering their dreams to God while keeping a level head as you guide them to achieve. One high school teacher put it perfectly one day when she said to Mario, "Tell me what you would do if the NBA is busy that year." He was taken aback by the question, but she was trying to tell him not to stop work on his education and to develop other dreams along the way, just in case. Mario's response, by the way, was "I guess something in politics." (Apparently God knew he was better suited to run up and down a basketball court than to run for office!)

In helping shape the dream, sometimes all we can do as parents is offer encouragement and guide our children to people who are willing to help them reach their dreams. Teach your children to recognize dream givers and dream takers. But more than that, teach them to believe in something bigger than themselves by providing them opportunities to serve others, even if it is just in your home. And, of course, teach them to never underestimate the power of prayer, hard work, dedication and perseverance.

At this point in my life I have not stopped dreaming for myself, and I pray I never do. One dream that will never change, is to continue to have the opportunity to watch my children live their dreams. Watching Mario's lifetime of hard work pay off as he competes in the NBA, and Roneka's career moves that have allowed her to live out her passions, are dreams come true for me. And I look forward to watching them continue to dream, as Mario works to achieve a whole new set of goals and as Roneka makes a career change in order to allow her next dreams to come true. As for how these dreams will come to fruition, I do not know, but I look forward to seeing it all unfold.

CELEBRATING THE JOYS

"If you can react the same way to winning and losing, that is a big accomplishment. That quality is important because it stays with you the rest of your life."

Chris Evert

While our children rely on us for direction (and sometimes correction) in order to grow and learn while under our care, our children also rely heavily on us to be their Number One Fan. A child's confidence comes foremost from the people who love him and cheer him on in every success, no matter how big or small. This is easy to do when your baby is still a baby, giving you that first smile or coo. Do you remember the first time your child rolled over? The first time your child ate a whole spoonful of cereal without spitting it back out? Took their first step or spoke their first word? You likely cheered like crazy for your little baby at each of those milestones.

The road from baby to toddler to adolescent is lined with so much achievement. Mastering major steps to independence, like walking, quickly generates praise and joy. The beaming pride and honest smile on a young child's face after learning to read or ride a bike make it easy to remember to celebrate the moment.

As they grow, however, remembering to be a fan is not always easy. Ideally, our children will rely less and less on us to do things for them and with them. This growing independence is natural, but can make a mother feel less important to her child with the passage of time. By the time they reach adolescence, you may be convinced they will never again want a congratulatory hug or high-five, or even acknowledgement from you.

Don't fall for it.

Your child will always, at any age, need you to celebrate. These celebrations, no matter how big or small, lift up and give validation to their joys, and it is important to continue these rituals of celebration whether your child is seven months or 17 years old. The impact of encouragement never gets smaller, even as your child gets bigger. After all, God is there with us celebrating every joy along every step of our own journey; our children always need that same gift from us.

While coaching basketball for teenage girls in Alaska, all too often I saw their heartbreak when they would turn to celebrate their achievements with someone only to be stung by loneliness. It didn't take a genius to realize that some of my teenage players hadn't had anyone validate their accomplishments in a very long time. It wasn't necessarily that they lacked people in their lives who loved them; they seemed to lack people ready and waiting to cheer them on. These girls were starving for someone to recognize their talents, drive and inner beings.

Many did not feel as though they had anyone who would share in their joy when they made "the shot," or anyone to lend a "great job" when they brought home an "A" on a report card.

These girls, like so many other kids, shined their lights bright and beautiful, but without someone willing to enjoy their glow, their lights quickly grew dim. As I watched these girls grow into adulthood without the kind of praise and recognition they longed for, I realized how important it is to cheer not only my own children, but all children. You never know what kind of impact that "Way to go!" or "You did great!" is going to have on a child, but I can assure you its value is priceless, and your own joys are multiplied.

> *"Therefore encourage one another and build*
> *one another up, just as you are doing."*
>
> *I Thessalonians 5:11*

As you reach out to lift up the children of others, you will find even greater appreciation for those who reach out to lift up your children, too. I have witnessed this to very different extremes with my own children, cheering them on with dozens, hundreds, and even thousands of people at various events over the years, with pride and joy at each and every one.

It was an especially interesting reality to watch my child's achievements take center stage in the national spotlight. I feel extremely blessed that so many of Mario's happiest moments have been celebrated by literally thousands upon thousands of people and that he has been able to bring joy to others, including his mother–as his basketball career progressed from his early days of playing ball with his friends.

The highs and lows of high school basketball in Alaska are not unlike those in any other state, with the exception of the longer nights and colder days. The seasons are filled with pep rallies and rivalries, heartbreak and celebrations. Local papers and news stations spotlight the teams and their star players, giving their communities something to be excited about for the winter, and giving the athletes' parents plenty of material for scrapbooking.

While still in high school, Mario received growing attention from colleges across the country, opening doors to many opportunities. He had worked hard and possessed the natural skill set to stand out among the best players in the state. Mario and Ronnie took a trip during Mario's junior year to the 2004 Final Four in San Antonio. That trip would inspire something very special four years later. Not knowing that the Final Four would be back in San Antonio while he was in college, and being blown away by the energy in the Alamodome, Mario leaned over to his dad during that game and told him, "I'll be back here one day playing for this!"

Boxing and that at turner stadium when he pitched!

I watched that prophecy come true with great awe, amazed at God's hand in a journey that ended up taking our family from North Carolina to Alaska to Kansas. I'll be honest: having grown up in North Carolina, I always secretly hoped Mario would end up a Carolina Tar Heel. North Carolina has a long-standing tradition of excellence in college basketball, and Coach Roy Williams is regarded as one of the greatest college coaches of all time. But most of all, knowing we would likely leave Alaska to be closer to our children after Mario's high school graduation, I liked the possibility of being able to settle back "home" in North Carolina. God had planned otherwise, however, and that plan included moving the Chalmers family to Lawrence, Kansas, home of the University of Kansas Jayhawks, where Mario would play for another very skilled coach, Bill Self. Like North Carolina, Kansas has a long and illustrious basketball reputation that dates back more than a century.

Interestingly, the relationship between Kansas and North Carolina runs long and deep. Roy Williams had coached at Kansas for 15 years before leaving to lead the Tar Heels, a move that took place only a few years before Mario became a Jayhawk, and a move that left a sting in the hearts of many Kansas fans. Before coaching at Kansas, Williams had been an assistant under Dean Smith at North Carolina, where he played ball as a college student. Ironically, before Smith coached for North Carolina, he played ball in college for Kansas, tying Kansas and North Carolina together in a very unique way. Basketball is not a pastime at either school, it is a passion.

Mario's first two years at Kansas brought many challenges and celebrations. It is a big jump from even the most memorable of high school games to Division I NCAA basketball. We were overwhelmed by the excitement surrounding each game; the thrill of playing at the legendary Allen Fieldhouse is like no other. Talk about sharing joy with others! Sitting among 16,000 fans, who don't stop cheering from the time the team hits the court until well after the final buzzer, is exhilarating! Under Coach Self, Mario learned not only to be a better player, but the joys of growing as part of a team. And for Mario, that team included his father. Ronnie took on the role of Director of Basketball Operations for the team when we moved to Lawrence.

During our first two years in Lawrence, I learned of the strong bond between the Jayhawk Nation and their beloved basketball team. I met alumni and fans from all over the country that glowed when the conversation turned to the 1950s and Wilt "The Stilt" Chamberlain, or "Danny and the Miracles" of 1988, the last year Kansas had won a national title. I heard stories of students camping outside of Allen Fieldhouse for days in the middle of winter just to be able to get the best seats available in the student section for big games. We were happy to be a part of the Jayhawk family.

By the beginning of Mario's third season, I understood fully that the University of Kansas was a global community that drew tremendous joy from their basketball team and the rich traditions associated with being a Jayhawk. And, as the new season began, I believed this team had the experience and drive to make great things happen.

That season, 2007-2008, was an exciting one, filled with much success and joy. Mario had appeared on the cover of *Sports Illustrated* before the season began, and seemed to be living up to the expectations put upon him by the public. His high stats and some very memorable plays drove the crowd nuts with enthusiasm. And, just as we had for the first two years, the Chalmers family all had our places at these games: Ronnie on the sidelines, Mario on the court and me in the stands, often with Roneka, who made the trip to see her little brother play as often as possible.

Kansas finished the regular season with a record of 28-3, first place in the Big 12 Conference. Mario scored a career-high 30 points in helping Kansas defeat the University of Texas to win the conference tournament, securing a number one seed for the Jayhawks in the NCAA Tournament.

Throughout my time in Lawrence, I had a wonderful circle of women from my Bible study who I knew I could count on to be a part of my team of prayer warriors. My friends were always quick to pray for our team's health and safety, and for our burdens to be lifted to God. Without their prayers and support, this journey would not have been so full of the peace and joy we had through all of its ups and downs. As the team prepared to begin the Big Dance of the NCAA Tournament, I carried my warriors and the calming spirit of their prayers in my heart into each of the next six games.

The first weekend of the tournament took us to Detroit, where Kansas played Portland State. The entire team gelled together with baskets evenly spread, leading Kansas to an 85-61 win. Two days later, Kansas advanced to the Sweet 16 with another well-balanced win, this time over UNLV, 75-56.

Two down, four to go.

The next weekend proved to be a little more challenging. Kansas dismantled Villanova 72-57 with a true team effort, and advanced to the Elite Eight where they were met by a hugely underestimated Davidson College. The game got off to a slow start, with both teams struggling to make plays. There were many lead changes and many nerve-wracking moments. With 16 seconds left in the game, Kansas was up by two and Davidson had the ball. Davidson set a play and launched a 3-point-shot to win the game at the final second, but the ball sailed left of the basket.

Four down, two to go. The Jayhawks were headed for the Final Four, at the Alamodome in San Antonio.

Sometimes, as parents we listen to our kids share their hopes and dreams, and while encouraging and guiding them to achieve those dreams, we wonder somewhere in the backs of our minds if our kids are setting themselves up for disappointment, and if our encouragement is only furthering that possibility. Other times we know, somewhere in the depths of our hearts, that those dreams are very likely to come true.

Mario was determined to play in the Final Four in San Antonio ever since attending the game there four years earlier with his dad. Now he was there, his goal had been reached. We were already celebrating before the last two games were even played.

In Jayhawk country, however, the celebration had very different full-circle significance. Not only was Kansas in the Final Four with a shot at bringing home the national title for the first time in exactly 20 years, but Kansas was going to have to play Roy Williams and his Tar Heels to get there.

Even some of my most God-loving friends seethed at the idea of losing this game to Kansas' former coach, such was the feeling of betrayal felt by so many when Williams left Kansas for his alma mater. This feeling, at times, seemed to cast a shadow over the excitement of reaching the Final Four.

Fortunately, the players did not see things that way. The players on this Kansas team had no ties to Coach Williams, only respect for the program at North Carolina, and a sincere understanding that the team they were about to play was, at that moment, ranked the best in the nation. The Jayhawk players had worked hard all year for this moment, a moment much greater than revenge. For the athletes on this team, the prospect of reaching a life-long goal was the only motivation they needed.

We arrived in San Antonio that first week in April to a flock of cheering Jayhawk fans. Everywhere we turned, there was another fan offering encouragement. "Go get them!" and "No mercy!" seemed to be the running soundtrack of those first couple of days.

The mother in me was nervous, and the coach in me could not stop analyzing. In my mind, I tried to match the opposing players skill-for-skill, and I tried to block out the doubtful voices. I asked Mario if he thought they could win. "Yeah," he replied, "I think we can win, Mom."

This was a huge weekend. Our team was about to play the biggest game of their lives so far, in the biggest venue they had ever played in, and, understandably, some of them were starting to grow anxious. I recall a conversation with one player, a wonderful young man deeply rooted in faith, who found his nerves getting the best of him. We talked for awhile about the enormity of the weekend and the power of God, and then I offered him a scripture reading that embodied the entire season and became a point of focus for the rest of the weekend.

"Have I not commanded you? Be strong and courageous. Do not be terrified; do not be discouraged, for the Lord your God will be with you wherever you go."

Joshua 1:9

Coach Chalmers (Ronnie) returned to our hotel room to get ready for the game after a team meeting. He was always a reliable pulse for the team, and I could tell from his beat that this team was confident. Later that evening, the Jayhawks came out onto the court and pounded away at the Tar Heels. Kansas took a strong and early lead, and in spite of a nerve-wracking lull in scoring during the second half, soundly beat North Carolina 84-66.

Five down, and we were left with one more task: beat the Memphis Tigers to bring home the national title that had eluded Kansas for 20 years.

After a day of rest and recuperation on Sunday, I awoke thoroughly refreshed on Monday morning, April 7, 2008, to a beautiful day in San Antonio. With my prayer warriors back in

Kansas, just a phone call away, I started the day ready to receive whatever God had in store. I just wished I knew what that was!

I sent Mario my usual pre-game text, a scripture followed by "LUV U," and he responded with his usual "LUV U 2." Ronnie was in and out of the room all morning with different meetings. He was a big ball of energy and, quite frankly, getting on my nerves. But I was not the only one.

"Almarie, I just don't know," he opened up, "Mario told me to leave him alone!"

I understood full well what Mario was saying. He could not handle his father's nervous energy on top of his own. I let Ronnie vent a bit more before he finally took a nap. After making sure my prayers for him to fall asleep had worked, I slipped into the next room for a chamomile tea and some time with God. I asked God to give me some words for peace. He answered with:

"For I know the plans I have for you, declares the Lord, plans to prosper you and not to harm you, plans to give you hope and a future. Then you will come upon me and come and pray to me, and I will listen to you."

Jeremiah 29:11

my mom's Vurse

Something about that verse resonated deep within me, so I copied it onto a slip of the hotel's note paper and continued in prayer. While sitting in the quiet room, I also talked with my dear friend and prayer warrior, Tandy, who had called me from

Lawrence to find out what prayer requests she could pass along to the Lawrence warriors for the day.

"Pray for Ronnie, Mario, the coaches, and for all of our guys to stay focused, with no spirit of fear," I asked her. But something inside of me felt incomplete with that prayer. I had never, in any of my years of playing, coaching, or mothering, prayed specifically for my team to win a game, and I was not about to start at that moment. But there was another prayer in my heart that left me feeling a bit selfish for even thinking of it.

"Tandy," I started, "would I sound selfish if I asked you to pray that Mario has a special moment at some point during this game? I don't always ask prayers for my son, but this game has such significance." I explained to Tandy how Mario had come so alive here, four years earlier, while sitting in the stands with his dad, telling his dad he would one day be back here playing in this game.

Like a gift from heaven, Tandy told me there was absolutely nothing wrong with praying for my child to have a special moment. Our children are given to us by God to care for and nurture. We are their number one cheerleaders and we are the first people called to pray for them. Of course we can pray for their shining moments to happen! "I'll be in prayer with you," she said, "that God will give him a little special moment."

We hung up with each other, and I settled into prayer in the silent stillness of my hotel room. It did not take long for me to feel God's presence wrapped around me. As I sat in the silence, scriptures came pouring into my mind. I wrote them down on a Hyatt notepad.

"The joy of the Lord is your strength."

Nehemiah 8:10

"Every place that the sole of your foot will tread upon I have given to you."

Joshua 1:3

I shared these scriptures with my husband just before he left for the final pre-game meeting, and he came back to the room a little while later with a grin. "I think we're ready," he said. I gave him the hotel note paper with the scriptures on it to keep in his pocket, and with Roneka, we made our way to our places at the Alamodome: Ronnie on the bench, Mario on the court, and Roneka with me in the stands.

I would love to say that I felt calm, cool, and confident without wavering from the moment I entered the building, but that would be a bit of a lie. Sure, I felt the calming spirit of God and knew He was there with us all. I tried to keep cool and was confident this would be a great game, but every now and then, I would feel my breath shorten or my stomach knot up. That is when I would reach into my pocket and pull out the scripture I had written down earlier to keep throughout the day and found it brought me instant peace:

"I know the plans I have for you…"

With Roneka on one side, and my friend, Robin, on the other, I was surrounded by good people. Robin's husband, Scott, was the team's academic advisor. Scott's strength, determination, and care had always been an inspiration for the team, and Robin's calm and kind spirit was exactly what I needed by my side. I also had invited another set of wonderful friends and prayer warriors, Lavonne and Julian, who felt this was an assignment; to be on stage, offering up prayers and support for what was a special moment for them as well.

And the game began.

To anyone who believes God is not present on an athletic court or field, I will tell you this: God might not pick favorites, but His presence can be present in every athlete striving to do their best. Any mother who has ever watched her son finally hit a baseball after umpteen tries at bat, or who has watched her daughter finally get her first volleyball serve over the net after nearly an entire season of learning how, and has seen the joy on that child's face and felt the spirit of confidence and self-worth that came from those successes, will tell you that God is there. You just need to look for Him.

So it was with that spirit that I watched a play early on, when Memphis was leading by four. Mario saved a loose ball that nearly went out of bounds and dished it to his teammate for a slam dunk, and I saw God answering my prayer. My son beamed with joy. He was having a blast, living out his dream, playing the game of his life. Knowing my prayer for Mario had been answered and that he had had his special moment, a fun memory all his own for the game, I was able to fully focus on the rest of the game as a whole.

It was a terrific game, one of the best in tournament history, with many lead changes and highlight-worthy plays. By halftime, the Kansas Jayhawks were up five, but that lead quickly diminished as the Memphis Tigers came back out fighting. We watched both teams work hard for every hoop. A three-pointer by Memphis was reviewed late in the second half when referees disagreed on the call. After reviewing the shot at the officiating table, the shot was called a two-pointer because the shooter's foot was inside the three-point arc. No one knew at the time how important that call would be.

As the clock wound down, Kansas started falling behind. Not apart, just behind. Nine points behind, to be exact, with 2:12 to go. As I said before, I had never in my life prayed for a victory, but at that moment, I will admit, I turned my head to heaven and said, "God, all I'm asking for is nine points, and I know that's nothing to you! I don't know how you are going to work this out, but could you just do it?"

"I know the plans I have for you…"

Just then a transformation began to take place. Memphis missed some key free throws and Kansas made some. Kansas made some key steals and the team capitalized on them. With :03.9 left on the clock and up by two, Memphis went to the foul line again. Their player missed the first shot and made the second, putting them up by three.

The clock began to tick. Sherron Collins brought the ball down the court for Kansas with great determination. After almost losing the ball, he dished it to Mario with :02.1 left. Mario, standing well-guarded outside the three-point line, released a game-tying shot that sailed toward the hoop in slow motion. As soon as that ball left his hands, I knew the plans too.

Nothing but net!

The world seemed to stop moving. I was standing up with my hands on my face, Coach Self's mother and wife turned and looked at me, the arena exploded in cheers. As excited as I was by the game going into overtime, I was not in awe because Mario had made the shot. I was in awe of God's answer to my prayer for my son. ***"Oh, my, God, You showed up and showed out!"*** I thought to myself, spellbound by the fact that God would use Mario for a time such as this. And of course, by the fact that we were heading into overtime. As Ronnie frequently says, the team that sends the game into overtime often wins.

Fueled by that comeback, Kansas went on to win the game, 75-68. Coach Bill Self had his first national title, and the Jayhawks had a whole new reason to celebrate. But even more than the shot or the win, I will always remember Mario giving thanks to God right there on the court as the final buzzer sounded to kick off the celebration.

> *"A man's gift maketh room for him and*
> *bringeth him before great men."*
>
> *Proverbs 18:16*

75

After celebrating with the team, Mario stole away and looked into the stands where I had been watching. Not finding me there (I was making my way down to the court), he found his sister, Roneka, and motioned "Where is Mom?" Roneka pointed to where I was heading and as we met we shared in the joy of the moment, hugging and tearing up as he gave me the biggest hug of a lifetime. "Mom we did it!" he said in an excited voice. So many people would tell me afterward that "the hug" was almost as special to watch as "the shot." And I am happy our own celebration could add such joy to that of others.

At that moment, I knew what a win meant to the team, and knew it would mean something special to the fans, but it was not until I returned to Lawrence and heard from friends and fans that I realized the full impact of the game. Winning a Final Four after 20 years is thrilling enough for a town that lives and breathes the sport, but winning in such dramatic fashion brought that thrill to a whole different level. Neighbors who had hardly ever spoken before found themselves connecting over that moment. Long-lost friends reconnected that night and in the days that followed. The impact on the local economy was a huge blessing. Restaurants and bars saw a tremendous boom in their business those weeks of the tournament. Apparel and souvenir shops exponentially increased their sales after the title game. Many folks told me they had prayed for Mario's shot to go in, and I could honestly tell them they were not alone! A general spirit of happiness blanketed the town of Lawrence and Jayhawk fans around the world.

It is impossible to put into words the feeling I have knowing how much joy the team's victory, and the shot by Mario, brought to so many in that one moment. But with all the attention, both good and bad, he receives from others, I can never forget that the "Way to go!" *that comes from his parents*, will always outweigh everything else he hears from his fans.

Resting in Him

"I know God will not give me anything I can't handle.
I just wish that He didn't trust me so much."

Mother Theresa

As mothers, there are so many things we celebrate with our children, from birthdays to first teeth to great report cards. Celebrating is the easy part, but it takes a lot of patience, love and sacrifice to get to a place of celebration. The journey to celebration requires us to rest in God's hands and seek His peace even when situations look hopeless.

If you think back on Mary, the mother of Jesus, she often had reason to celebrate. Her son healed people, performed miracles and taught others the right way to live. Imagine her joy when people talked about Him. But on the other hand, she also experienced the lows of motherhood when she had to truly trust God for strength. Imagine her anguish when her son was nailed to the cross. I am sure that she rested in God's hands to get through that terrible time in her life. Her son had a calling and she played a big role in getting Him prepared for it. Maybe the biggest part she played was giving birth and knowing that on the path of his life would go forth with or without her approval.

All of our children have a calling in their lives. Maybe it is to help others as a doctor, to encourage others as a teacher, coach, minister or lawyer, or to be a role model for children who desperately need one. Whatever it is, we need to remember to celebrate the good times and to stand firm in the bad times, because both come with the journey.

My deepest desire as we travel the road of Mario playing in the NBA, is that our entire family will always stay humble and understand that this is a higher calling. I remind myself and our family often that "to whom much is given, much is required." It is great to make it, but one must stay focused, work hard and be diligent while on the journey, because when we are given much, we often take it for granted.

Staying grounded in the middle of high-profile situations and the accompanying media hype can be nearly impossible, but in order to truly find the joy in our God-given journey, we must stay focused. This isn't about Mario Chalmers, he was just chosen for the journey. Yes, God wants us to celebrate the joys that we experience along the way, but humbly.

This goes for all of us, not just ballplayers on the big court, but Little Leaguers, pageant contestants, scouts, musicians, artists, actors, choir girls or boys or on whatever path your child excels. God gives us these joys and He wants us to teach our children that it is not all about them; it is about the experience He has given them to make an impact in the arena in which they stand.

"Taste and see that the Lord is good.
Blessed is the man who trusts and takes refuge in Him."

Psalm 34:8

Joy is defined in the dictionary as "the emotion of great delight or happiness caused by something exceptionally good or satisfying; keen pleasure; elation." I believe that when we celebrate our children's victories, as well as our own, we should do so with a spirit of gratefulness and elation, not in an "I did it on my own" kind of way. Because as the Bible tells us "pride cometh before a fall." I do think that God wants us to feel good about our success, but He also wants us to acknowledge His role in it and to know without divine intervention some things may not be possible

Believe it or not, I find it harder to celebrate my children's successes now than I did when they were winning relay races in elementary school, and I think it all goes back to that pride and humility issue. But as the journey continues, I strive to learn to celebrate and appreciate, while remaining a good role model and representative to others who have yet to cross this path.

"He leads the humble in doing right, teaching them his way."

Psalm 25:9

While it appears that I have even more reason to celebrate now, I try hard not to allow outside influences dampen my joy. You see, on the one hand, I want people to know that even in the midst of all the hype, I am a normal mother who reacts and deals with everyday situations. However, sometimes if you aren't watchful you can get so busy trying to prove that you are down to earth, that you don't give yourself the opportunity to celebrate your children's successes. I am careful not to be perceived as acting like I have arrived, or that I have all of the parenting answers. This isn't realistic, and in life it is all about the journey. We learn various lessons each day. I know that I certainly want to stay humble along the way and be a blessing to others as I pass on the lessons I've learned.

I am still learning to embrace the joy of the journey. And I want to encourage you to work on doing the same, as you let God plan your family's voyage. Of course, in our minds, we map out our perfect journey, but oftentimes, life doesn't follow our plan. When we have a small child our "perfect plan" may look something like this: our child will go to the best pre-school, skip a grade in elementary school, be popular in junior high and be the star of the high school team.

When we set our own goals, and don't rely on wisdom as we make our plans, we are setting ourselves up for heartache and headaches along the path. Even when we do have wisdom, bumps in the road are still inevitable. It is during these bumpy times that we have to find solace and peace in God's divine plan. I am reminded daily that Christ gives peace and rest to all who come to Him in faith. The limelight comes with so many joys, but it also casts a beacon on mistakes and bad choices. See, I know that even though expectations are placed on those who are front and center, they may stumble sometimes because they make the wrong choices and they are human. But God forgives the well-known, just like He does the unknown. His journey doesn't stop because we sin; He forgives us and loves us through it all.

> *"You will guard him and keep him in perfect and constant peace, whose mind (both its inclination and its character) is stayed on You, because he commits himself to You, leans on You, and hope confidently in You. Trust in the Lord forever, for the Lord, the Lord, is the Rock eternal."*
>
> *Isaiah 26:3-4*

What God has planned for my family is specifically designed with us in mind, but He also has a unique plan for your family. Finding that plan means lining yourselves up with God's will and staying focused on Him even when you aren't sure that you are on the right path or when things go wrong. Admittedly, resting in God in these times can be very difficult, especially when it comes to our children, but that is yet another part of the faith walk in life.

I remember a time when I desperately wanted to celebrate the joy of my daughter's 21st birthday with her, but was too far away. I felt relieved that the young man whom she was dating while away at college had planned to take her out for a celebration dinner. However, when the time came for him to pick her up, he was nowhere to be found. In fact, the whole night passed and he never showed up. She called with disappointment in her voice, and I wanted nothing more than to board a plane and go "rescue her." However, I couldn't get from Alaska to North Carolina that quickly, so I had to remain in God's rest. Instead of rushing off to her side, all I could do was give her sound advice. I told her to celebrate the fact that God may have saved her from a long-term situation, by letting her see this young man's true colors early on. I also told her that in the future, she should make party plans and invite the guests herself so that she doesn't have to rely on anyone else to create special moments for her.

There have been similar times with Mario when he has had an off game or missed a game-winning shot, when I must rest in God's hands. The fact that there is widespread media coverage of his performances—both good and bad—makes these moments especially difficult. I have to remember that my God knows the plans as well as the lesson to be taught. Our loving God is sure to give us more joys to celebrate, but at times like this, we are learning that life really is out of our control.

These examples may seem trivial, but there have been and will be many more major life altering events that teach all of us to rest in His arms. At times we will experience the death of a loved one, or perhaps divorce for ourselves or our children, disease or tragedy, but through these times we learn that resting in Him requires that we trust in God's perfect and divine plan. He knows the end before the beginning. In trying situations, we must encourage our children, as well as ourselves, to stay focused and do our part, and allow God to do the rest.

I encourage all mothers to find scriptures that you can reflect on when times seem too hard to bear. Steal away to quietness, even if it is just in the shower (which, by the way, can be a wonderful prayer closet). Renew your strength and confidence on a daily basis whether you are resting in Him or celebrating the joys. It is during these times that you must rest and regain your confidence in Him. Take time out to be still and quiet, surround yourself with other believers, stand on your word, listen to music that encourages the spirit, exercise, continue to stand, pray and ask for what you need, as you trust God!

Here's a hard lesson in learning to rely on Him: God's ways aren't always our ways, His timing isn't always our timing, but I have found that His way is the best way.

"We are assured and know that all things work together and are (fitting into a plan) for good to and for those who love God and are called according to (His) design and purpose."

Romans 8:28

We all watch our children go through tough, challenging and rebellious times. God calls us to keep praying, even when we don't understand. Take a bold stand as needed, and pray that they learn the lesson as you travel the journey with, beside or behind them. It is important that they know that you are there. Often it is your presence that speaks greater volume than your words in those trying times. Encourage your children to stay the course until you know that they have come to the end of the journey. Then it is time to allow them to travel on, remembering that God holds the divine plan.

> *"For his anger lasts only a moment, but his favor*
> *lasts a lifetime! Weeping may last through the*
> *night, but joy comes with the morning."*
>
> *Psalm 30:5*

I thank God that He has supplied my needs and will continue to do so as I trust Him in the next season of my journey. We must always trust that small still voice that speaks from within. He has a journey planned for us. It may be bumpy sometimes, but it will be wrapped in joy as His arms carry us all the way!

THE ART OF LETTING GO

"Letting go is one way of saying I love you."

Unknown

Every stage of motherhood has its struggles, and I'm not sure that we ever really "master" any of the stages before moving on to the next chaotic place that life takes us. However, I'm absolutely positive of one thing: letting go is one stage that is hard to learn and, honestly, I wonder if it is entirely impossible!

I write this as I sit exchanging text messages with Mario and Roneka. They are keeping me informed about their flight schedules as they each travel to various parts of the world. What happened to my little darlings who came and crawled up in my lap for a bedtime story? My prayers were fervent for them then, but even more so now.

In the journey of being the parent of adult children, the prayers are constant for a variety of things (i.e. God-centeredness, safety, job success, good health, connecting with the right spouse and the list could go on). But I feel this is a part of parenthood. I believe prayer helps maintain peace and harmony within a family unit.

Yes, various issues can come into play with the many opportunities for trickery on this journey which makes me reflect on the story of Jacob and Esau, which speaks of sibling rivalry –another subject for another day. But read and reflect on the lesson to be learned about those brothers.

As mothers of young children, we can't help but visualize what it will be like when our children are grown. Will they want us around? Will we have a close relationship? I have recently realized that my struggle in learning to "let go" is really more about learning to parent in a different way. Yes, it may not mean knowing every little thing that goes on in their lives, but it does mean learning to leave that to their Heavenly Father while I continue my daily prayers for my children.

We often see parents characterized as the dreaded visitors or the butt of jokes on television shows, but it doesn't have to be that way. The adult child/parent relationship can be fulfilling and rewarding to both sides if the boundaries with each other are respected. Sometimes we are given the opportunity to share life experiences with our adult children, and other times we just get to watch as they go on the journey. When we aren't allowed in, it may sting a little, but I have found that praying for them helps ease that pain and helps me keep the right perspective on the relationship.

As I think back to when I was in my children's shoes, I can't imagine not having my grandmother to share in my life. I remember fondly the times I called her to share that I was pregnant, getting my first job or buying our first house. She would celebrate those times with me even when it was on the phone. Then there were the times when I just needed her to listen, as I struggled with bosses, teachers or even something as simple as finding a babysitter. No matter the situation, she was always available with a caring ear or a word of wisdom, encouragement and assurance that it would all work out. Even on those rocky days when I thought that my marriage was going to end, I would call her. She would just listen and encourage me to stick it out, which was exactly what I needed to hear at the time. She was not only my parent, but she had become a confidant, and a friend.

That is the beautiful part about this stage: I am no longer just a parent, now I can be a friend to my children. I encourage you to make and keep special times with your adult children. Keep birthday dinners a priority, but realize that they may happen before or after the actual date. If all are up for it, family vacations or gatherings can be an annual thing. There are so many things you can still do to build on your relationships as you operate within the boundaries of this new phase of your lives.

My prayer for all of us is that, regardless of what big or small successes are encountered, we remember why we are here. God put children in your lives for a reason. Even if the reason is part of the life's lesson. We must stay true to who we are and what we are called to do while living on this earth. For each of us the journey is different, but equally important in the sight of God. For He knows the plans He has for each of us. That plan may or may not include fortune or fame, but <u>whatever you do, you do in His name and</u> to bring glory to Him as well as touch the lives of others.

I often reflect on God's promise when He said, "Before I formed you in the womb I knew the plans…" (Jeremiah 1:5). Whatever we were born for, we are equipped to do. On those days when it may seem too difficult to bear, seek His face and listen to that still, small voice that is always there to lead and guide you along the way. We simply need to stay connected and trust that God is a <u>God who doesn't make mistakes.</u>

I remind you, as I remind myself often, to *be still and know that He is God* and remember He will never leave you, nor will He forsake you. Continue to seek His face, trust and follow His plan. It is one thing to say you trust and another one to truly walk the walk of trusting Him. Remember that if we do our part, God will certainly do His.

In writing this book I can say that it isn't a cure-all, or is it a guarantee that raising children using formula A, B or C will insure that they will do or get all things right. I was reminded of this fact as I sat engaging in conversation with a single mom who described her choice by saying "this isn't the path that my parents took, nor was it what I planned. Yes, we all make choices and some of those take us down roads that we haven't planned. I have decided that this is the path for my life and this isn't necessarily the right way in which it all happened, but I am choosing to embrace it as the path for me and think about the blessings vs. the other many thoughts that come to mind".

Very well spoken, I thought, as it pertained to her journey. I still like the message I learned while I was just a youngster from an old rhyme. It goes like this: First Comes Love, Then Comes Marriage and THEN comes _____ in the Baby Carriage!

In this journey of letting go, one must know that the responsibility should land on their shoulders, as it is their choices and decisions that make their path in life. The art of letting go, as it relates to our adult children, is recognizing that it is their lives, and we just get to walk along beside them, and offer guidance as requested, but I have learned that the choices they make are their own. Sometimes their choices aren't always easy on parents, especially when we have trained and taught them during those earlier years. However, I've gone back to the fact it's their life to live and I as well have a life to live; following my own path, which I must continue in the midst of it all.

Comments or questions may be directed to
Almarie at AlmarieSpeaks@gmail.com

CONCLUSION

The Parent's Tao Te Ching

Happiness is Contagious
If you always compare your children's abilities
to those of great athletes, entertainers, and celebrities,
they will lose their own power.
If you urge them to acquire and achieve,
they will learn to cheat and steal
to meet your expectations.

Encourage your children's deepest joys,
not their superficial desires. Praise their patience,
not their ambition.
Do not value the distractions and diversions
that masquerade as success.
They will learn to hear their own voice
instead of the noise of the crowd.
If you teach them to achieve
they will never be content.
If you teach them contentment,
they will naturally achieve everything.

We all want our children to be happy.
Somehow, some way today
show them something that makes you happy,
something you truly enjoy.
Your own happiness is contagious.
They learn the art from you.

William Martins

How can you use this book?

MOTIVATE

EDUCATE

THANK

INSPIRE

PROMOTE

CONNECT

Why have a custom version of *The Ball Is In Your Court*?

- Build personal bonds with customers, prospects, employees, donors, and key constituencies
- Develop a long-lasting reminder of your event, milestone, or celebration
- Provide a keepsake that inspires change in behavior and change in lives
- Deliver the ultimate "thank you" gift that remains on coffee tables and bookshelves
- Generate the "wow" factor

Books are thoughtful gifts that provide a genuine sentiment that other promotional items cannot express. They promote employee discussions and interaction, reinforce an event's meaning or location, and they make a lasting impression. Use your book to say "Thank You" and show people that you care.

The Ball Is In Your Court is available in bulk quantities and in customized versions at special discounts for corporate, institutional, and educational purposes. To learn more please contact our Special Sales team at:

1.866.775.1696•sales@advantageww.com•wwwAdvantageSpecialSales.com

Breinigsville, PA USA
04 February 2011
254852BV00002B/2/P

9 781599 322131